Want to start making real money from the Internet today! And become a Coffee Shop Millionaire.

This ebook is short and to the point it. Is not intended to be some step by step money making guide that doesn't teach you anything. No this is more of a guide for knowing some of the different way's there are to make a good passive income online.

It can be done if you just put in a little work as they say nothing in life is completely free you will have to do some up front work to get your system whatever you chose to do up and running.

I am not a millionaire and I don't have fancy cars I don't take long vacations. What I do is make money online and these are some ways that I do it. It is all up to how much money you want to make remember it can be done.

Passive internet income, Make money from Home, Making Money Online, The income power of blogging, Ways to Make Money from the Internet, Selling eBook's online, Affiliate marketing,

This ebook with work-from-home job opportunities was written and priced for anyone who needs access to real companies that pay you to work from the comfort of your home.

The economy is changing at an incredible rate and while many jobs are disappearing or being downsized, a world of new opportunities is exploding.

If you are unemployed or underemployed this concise guide will show you more than a few ways you can start making money online immediately with your computer and an internet connection.

Author Richard C.H. Yates Sr.

DISCLAIMER AND/OR LEGAL NOTICES

TOC

Ways to make money from the internet

1. Blogging

2. Paid writing

3. Affiliate marketing

4. e-tuitions

5. Buy/sell domains

6. GPT program

7. Online marketing

8. Making Themes

9. Selling Photos

10. Virtual assistant

11. You Tube

12. Researching for others

13. Building applications

14. Video Game testing

The income power of blogging

1. AdSense

2. Amazon Associates

3. Other similar affiliate programs

4. Sponsorships

5. E-books

6. Selling your own product

7. Selling blog advertisement space

8. monetizing your RSS feed

9. Sponsoring reviews

10. Membership

Easy Ways to Make Money on the Internet Work Less and Earn More: Ways to Earn Passive Income

Best Ways to Make Quick Money Online

Choose the Genuine Method

Choose your Niche

Selling Online

Providing Online Services

Coffee Shop Millionaire Review Earn Money with Freedom

Ways to make money from the internet

The internet has indeed proved to be a blessing for one and all. There is hardly anything that you cannot do using the internet, you can play games, watch movies, plan vacations, book tickets and even make money.

Yes, you can indeed earn a decent amount, and to help you get started below are given different ways to make money from the internet.

1. Blogging

If you are a passionate writer and want to be published but cannot find a way to do so, you can start penning your own blog and fulfill your desires.

To start a blog you do not need any extensive technical skills, but you must have great knowledge in the field you choose to write on.

This will help attract more and more visitors to your site. If you manage to build a large following, you can then earn profit by writing paid reviews or gain commission by promoting others' products.

2. Paid writing

Writing contents is one of the best ways to make money from the internet. Many sites need freelance writers to write for them.

You can write as many articles as you desire, on your chosen topic, and then get paid for them.

Selling eBook's online can also help you make money. Writing eBook's needs no investment and there are no printing and shipping costs involved.

3. Affiliate marketing

If you have a knack of selling, then affiliate marketing can help you make a decent sum. As an affiliate, you will earn money by promoting and selling products through your website.

You do not have to own that product, but just need to sign up with a company's affiliate program, and then sell products under your referral link.

4. e-tuitions

The need of tutors is rising day by day. So, if you think you can help others learn then e-learning can help you make money. You just need to sign up with an online tutorial website, choose your favorite subject, spare few hours per week helping students with their problems, and you get paid quite a good sum.

5. Buy/sell domains

You can buy and sell domains and make money from the comfort of your home. You can buy domains at cheap rates and then sell them for profit. Before buying domains make sure you do some research to know about the hottest selling names.

6. GPT program

Get-paid-to or GPT sites are becoming more and more popular. You need to sign up for free websites, newsletters, fill online surveys, or play games.

These are perfect ways to make money for those people, who do not have a particular skill set, and still wish to earn money online. Taking surveys online is very simple.

You just need to register with some genuine paid survey websites and fill in their survey forms. There are endless topics that you will come across. Though this cannot help you to make a living, but you can indeed earn some pocket money.

7. Online marketing

After a website is created and optimized for the search engine then the Search Engine Marketing or SEM starts.

An SEM/SEO expert has the responsibility of marketing a website and he can promote it in many different ways.

These include writing press release, article marketing, blog posting, forum posting, and submitting sites to search engines and directories and so on.

Most of the companies do not do it themselves and you can help them with this and make some good money.

8. Making Themes

With more and more people understanding the importance of online presence, the need for Word Press Blog and Website template themes will keep on increasing.

If you have enough expertise in website designing and coding then you can design web based themes and earn a lot of money.

9. Selling Photos

If you have good photography skills, then you can use this talent and make money. There are many people who might be interested in your photographs, and will pay you quite a good amount for them.

10. Virtual assistant

Small businesses do need help to manage their tasks, but might not want to hire a full-time employee. You can be hired as a virtual assistant and then take up the responsibility of a traditional assistant or secretary, but from the comfort of your home. You can expect to do work like make travel reservations, pay bills, and manage expense reimbursements and so on.

11. You Tube

YouTube definitely is there to entertain you, but have you ever noticed those that upload their videos in YouTube are people just like you.

If you are a comedian, musician or any other type of artist who needs a wider audience then you can upload your videos on YouTube.

You will enjoy earnings depending on the ads displayed on your video page. If you post a number of videos and each of them becomes successful, then you can also expect partnership with YouTube.

12. Researching for others

If you cannot write or design, you need not lose heart as you still can make money on the internet. If you are ready to spare few hours each week, and willing to work hard, then you can opt to do some simple research jobs.

There are people who need some research to be done but do not have time to do it all by themselves. This opportunity can help you make quite a good sum.

13. Building applications

With smartphones becoming so popular, their applications or apps are also gaining more and more popularity.

Google's Android Market has more than a million apps and iPhone has over 3 million apps. Most of them sell like crazy.

You can also develop and sell your own app and make money on the internet.

Apps cost you almost nothing and require no shipping cost or storage, so you can enjoy great profit margins.

14. Video Game testing

This is a fun filled job that helps you make some money too. Many companies keep developing new video games and they need people of different age groups to test it for them.

You just need to play the game, and report the company of any problem that you experienced. So, you can enjoy playing the game, while also getting paid for it.

The income power of blogging

Blogging is a famous, effective and great way of earning money online. In fact, if you use the right techniques, you earn so much money through blogging that you can even consider quitting your full-time job.

So if you too have a flair for writing, are imaginative and want to earn money through blogging, here is a rundown on the income power of blogging.

It has to be mentioned that there are various methods to employ to make money from blogging; it is generally better to try a few of the techniques to finally decide which technique generates the most revenue for you.

1. AdSense

Google's AdSense is the top pick for bloggers to generate money just by placing advertisements on the blog.

This is mainly because it is easy to use, and does not require you're having too much of technical know-how to use it. All you have to do to put an AdSense on your blog is to copy and paste the code.

As this is one of the biggest advertising networks around, you have a wide range of advertisers to work with. So if your blog is based on an obscure niche, AdSense will definitely help you earn money through your blog.

Using Google AdSense is in fact the easiest way to monetize your blog as it automatically scans your blog and places the related ad on your blog for free. You are then paid based on the number of clicks on ads your blog generates.

2. Amazon Associates

Through the Amazon Associates program, you earn a part of the sales generated by people who click through your blog and make a purchase on Amazon.

However you earn only when people buy something from Amazon; the amount is determined on what the people order and how many people make purchases via your link.

So this concept of earning money through blogs works best for people who have blogs that somehow focus on products and shopping as people will be in a shopping mood while visiting your site.

3. Other similar affiliate programs

 Besides Amazon's Affiliate programs, there are other programs you can take part in. based on the topic of your blog, and the amount of traffic the blog generates, you can participate in many marketing programs.

However as some marketing programs only want blogs that generate high traffic, you have to wait and build up your traffic before signing up for the program.

With the growth of your blog, you can earn money online by reaching out to the small companies whose products you trust and use to find out if they are interested in setting up an affiliate marketing program with you.

In such a case, you just have to post a link to their product on your blog and when a person clicks through your blog to their site to order and buy the product, you earn a portion of the sale. While there are many affiliate programs and websites you can approach and apply for, Clickbank is the best of the lot.

4. Sponsorships

On the contrary, as your blog grows in popularity, you can make money through private sponsorships and ads. However unlike AdSense ads that come to you, you have to go out and look for private ads, just like magazines approaching companies for placing ads on their pages.

To sell these private ads, you have to convince the company that your blog generates sufficient traffic and prove that your blog covers a topic that fits the product or service the company offers.

5. E-books

You provide free information to people through your blog. However you can expand on the information you offer to people by writing an e-book and selling it on your blog to make money.

As your e-book connects with the content of your blog, you have to somehow expand it as no one wants to pay for content that you had previously given away for free.

So if you have a cookery blog, you could write a short cookbook with some unpublished recipes that are not available elsewhere. You can also sell e-books written by others through your blog post, and earn a percentage of the sales generated for the e-books.

6. Selling your own product

One of the best ways to generate money through your blog is to discuss and share any product you have to sell. However just make sure you have merchant service to make this happen.

7. Selling blog advertisement space

Try making various advertisement spaces on your blog sized about 125 x 125, and selling these spaces through websites like buy/sell-ads.

It is up to you to determine the rate for selling your advertisement space, based on the size and popularity of your blog. You could perhaps charge about $5 - $20 per month for each piece of advertising space.

8. monetizing your RSS feed

This is another great option for making money through blogging. Here, when a visitor on your blog subscribes to your blog, you just send the visitor an email about your new post.

Then your visitor reaches your RSS feed wherein you can monetize your RSS using Google AdSense.

9. Sponsoring reviews

Bloggers consider this a great opportunity to easily make money. All you have to do is write a review for a product on your blog and you automatically earn money.

You can use help of the many online review networks like sponsoredreview.com and pay per post.com to make money this way.

10. Membership

Once your blog grows and has an established group of readers, you can make even more money by offering memberships to your blog.

Have people pay a yearly or monthly amount to gain access to some exclusive content on your blog, for participating in forums or to receive a monthly newsletter from you.

You could also start a members-only portion on your blog where readers feel special and you earn money in the process.

These are 10 of the most effective means of making money through blogging and your blog. However just remember that you need patience, and that you can't expect to become a millionaire overnight.

With focus and dedication, you will be able to slowly find and use the right techniques to bring out the exact income potential of blogging and your blog.

Easy Ways to Make Money on the Internet Work Less and Earn More: Ways to Earn Passive Income

Passive income means earning income by some means which doesn't involve direct participation of the person. This is indeed a very attractive offer for those who want to have a substantial income without working more.

Even though there is a need for some initial investment and some work at the beginning, after that it is possible to earn income without playing any active role in business.

This is somewhat like earning profit by being a sleeping partner in a business. If you are a shrewd business minded people, it is better to get involved in such a business.

A sleeping partner is the one who makes initial investments for any business organization and later doesn't take part in any event of that business.

This is especially suitable for those who have a huge amount of money to invest but not interested in business and other related risky things.

All that he can do is to start a business with his investments and allow someone who is trustworthy to him to carry on the business and get some share from the profits earned in that business.

Usually millionaires and billionaires use these techniques to increase their money by several folds.

Building luxurious homes and giving them to needy people on rent is another important way of earning passive income. This involves no other risks except initial investment made by person.

Building homes requires huge amount to be invested today, but as rents of homes are also increasing day by day, it is really a profitable business. There are some people in big cities that live alone on rents earned from rented homes.

Giving buildings for rent to shops, commercial enterprises and other big business enterprises is another important way of earning passive income.

As these commercial offices need more space than homes, there is a need for big buildings for running such enterprises. Initial investment is really very high, but there is no doubt that one can get huge rewards for what he has invested at first.

Writing a book is yet another way of earning passive income, even though it needs initial efforts. Writing a book is not a big thing, but writing it in such a way that publishers get attracted towards them and accept them is very important.

Publishers read each and every book carefully and decide whether people purchase that book or not and depending on its marketability, they pay royalty to author. This royalty may range between several millions to several billion dollars.

This money can be deposited in banks and one can live happily just by the interest paid by banks for that deposit. This is also a type of passive income.

Yes there is several online income earning methods which also help one to earn passive income. Creating a blog and getting a large number of visitors to that blog everyday attracts several Google AdSense advertisements and that earns a huge income to blogger.

Even though it needs some creativity to start blog and maintain it to ensure good traffic at the beginning, after it gains some popularity there is no doubt that new people keep visiting that blog and it earns huge income to blogger.

Best Ways to Make Quick Money Online

There are various methods available through which you can earn money fast through online. You need not have to put much effort for making lots of money through internet.

The best way through which you can do this is by making yourself engaged in some odd jobs, or by selling certain products or services. As usual being unique can only make you gain more money than others without much effort.

Choose the Genuine Method

When you are choosing an employer or when you are being part of a website that is available online and offers you to make money quickly over internet, you should make sure that you are with the right person.

There are many websites that are frauds and may not pay you after getting your work. The frauds also demands money from you for joining them .You should never be part of any such works that asks you to give money.

If somebody is in need of your service or your work, they will be paying you rather than asking you to pay. You should understand the scams over internet.

Before joining a particular programme for making money, it is better for you to make a good online research that can help you in gaining adequate amount of information about the company you are chosen to be part of.

It is better to avoid being part of the multi-level as well as pyramid kind of marketing. These kinds of marketing are meant for taking money from and there is less chance for such programs to benefit you.

Choose your Niche

There are various methods through which you can earn money by making use of internet. You should choose the way you want to earn money. It is better to choose a niche that is a part of your interest.

If you are interested in marketing, you can easily make money by selling your products. If you are intellectually good, then choose that path for making money.

Choosing the right track that is suitable for the skills and abilities you possess can make a greater difference over the income you make out of it.

After you have chosen your niche, you need to launch a website or start a blog or be part of the other website or blog for making it possible for you to make a good amount of income.

Selling Online

If the area of your interest is marketing then you can easily make it possible to sell various things online. You can advertise on the products that you are going to sell through online.

The products can be any stuff that you do not want. You can even sell you paintings, or some kind of art work.

This way of sales can bring lot of money to you in a quick manner. You can even sell things on auction.

Providing Online Services

If you are an intellectual then you can make a lot of money online by providing services like editing, writing, proof reading etc. to the clients that approach you over the internet.

Coffee Shop Millionaire Review Earn Money with Freedom

What is a coffee shop millionaire? Envision leaving your home each morning, portable computer under control, daily paper in the other.

You head down to your nearby cafe, request your $2 measure of Joe and get to work. Presently, envision doing this and winning $21 million. Unthinkable, you'd think, isn't that so? Not so.

That is precisely what Anthony Trister did. Utilizing simply his portable computer, his initiative and the free Wi-Fi in his nearby bistro, he fabricated a web business that got him twenty one million dollars.

So you have 21 million motivations to ask yourself, would I be able to be an espresso joint mogul? I can't answer that with a straightforward yes or no.

Some individuals are removed to be moguls and some are definitely not. Destined to be, shake strong moguls, and have one thing that truly separates them.

They have, initially, the longing, and second, the stamina to drive forward, to study all the traps of the exchange and to continue taking those first steps, considerably after a fall. I know this is all threadbare psycho-jibber jabber. Anyhow it's correct.

Assuming that you need to be some piece of the new era of moguls, the cafe mogul who makes his fortune on the go, you truly require the longing and the readiness to study.

There are some plans. You can begin with become a Coffee Shop Millionaire, program. The precise first one is the money machine program that is partitioned further into 4 more segments.

The foremost segment of the money machine is neighborhood money machine which tells about how you can gain cash with nearby web markets or corners.

However, the arrangement is not exclusively for the individuals close neighborhood business as all your business methodology is dependent upon web correspondence.

An alternate money machine is the update. An update money machine tells the part of espresso joint tycoon program about how you can procure greater measure of cash by simply sending the limited time message and updates to the clients and potential clients.

An article money machine might be the best choice to research the article showcasing systems.

The article showcasing is for the most part concerned an arrangement with customer who might pay you for composing the special articles yet if there should arise an occurrence of happening with espresso bar tycoon, you might need to strive for no customer and it would truly be a simple errand to acquire greatest measure of cash.

The principal step is to get your-self in there, as close as could be expected under the circumstances to the individuals who have walked the walk.

That means joining a program that will show you the ropes and all the insider traps of the exchange.

Attempting to do only it, is including years of exertion through experimentation, that you can totally remove in the event that you snare with someone who has as of recently got there.

The great news is that there are truly many projects that show you how to turn into a cafe tycoon, yet just, perhaps twelve, that worth their salt. I prescribe two projects, the first is undoubtedly

"Google Sniper", an incredible choice for amateurs and provided that you're even a smidge acquainted with how Internet advertising functions or maybe only a learner how enjoys a test, and I suggest the amazing, Coffee Shop Millionaire project by Anthony Trister himself.

It might be a perfect working situation, provided that you might not need to answer your supervisor, you might have adaptable working hours and you might have the capacity to acquire better than average cash without putting much exertion.

With a specific end goal to carry on with that great life of flexibility, you might need to turn into a fruitful ambitious person.

You might need to manufacture your online business in a manner that it might be working like a self-recreating framework to create a ceaseless stream of salary for you.

There are gigantic numbers of items accessible in business sector guaranteeing to make you tycoon in not many days, assuming that you are looking to make that self-repeating framework.

Shockingly, the vast majorities of these aforementioned items are a trick or over-evaluated to make a fake buildup of that item through paid notices. Hence, I have been doing research about it and uncovered an answer as Coffee Shop Millionaire.

It is a most ideal approach to make that self-imitating framework to give you a bordering stream of a not too bad salary.

In this article, I will audit this item to carry out every last bit of its sure and negative focuses. I have watched through my experience.

Most importantly, becoming a Coffee Shop Millionaire is not one of the aforementioned traps to make you mogul in not many days.

Rather, it is about making a lifestyle of supreme flexibility, where you can live wherever you need and work wherever and at whatever point you need to work without being liable to anybody.

It is a complete item having devices; preparing and orderly direction to kick you off regardless of provided that you are a learner, halfway or progressed master searching for better approaches to profit on the web.

Regardless of where you are and what you are, Coffee Shop Millionaire holds a few approaches to help you to win full-time pay on the web.

Particularly, it is proposed to experience its eight weeks of preparing from Six Figure Secrets Club and $21k System.

These two ranges particularly satisfy its guarantee to show you how to profit online rapidly.

Assuming that you will center in these two zones, Coffee Shop Millionaire will disobediently give some productive outcomes.

We have discussed its pure focus, now how about we observe the imperfections. It has been watched that Coffee Shop Millionaire has barely an excessive amount of data to handle in the event that you are a fledgling.

Provided that its item preparing and instruments might have been more directional for apprentices, it might have been way more viable.

Assuming that I might need to give convincing comments about this item, I might say, in the event that you might use every last bit of its devices and preparing legitimately, it could be advantageous for you to win cash on the web.

Then again, provided that you might attempt to try different things with it, Coffee Shop Millionaire may not work for you.

I can essentially make sure that with either of these systems, you'll study everything you have to be the fruitful. Recollect, .Remember, all millionaires started by taking the first steps.

That is the most essential thing you've got to do however to be additional certain you're going in the right bearing, which is immeasurably imperative, investigate the projects I've suggested and I'll see you sometime in the coffee shop!